Hey World, Here I Am!

JEAN LITTLE

Hey World,
Here I Am!

Illustrations by
Barbara Di Lella

KIDS CAN PRESS
TORONTO

Acknowledgment

My sincere thanks go to David Booth
who liked Kate's poems enough
to show them to the people
at Kids Can Press.

Canadian Cataloguing in Publication Data

Little, Jean, 1932-
  Hey World, Here I Am!

Poems.
ISBN 0-921103-14-X (bound)
ISBN 0-919964-71-0 (pbk)

1. Children's poetry, Canadian (English)*.
I. Di Lella, Barbara. II. Title.

PS8523.I87H49 1986   jC811'.54   C86-093766-6
PZ8.3.L57He 1986

Kids Can Press Ltd. acknowledges with appreciation the
assistance of the Canada Council and the Ontario Arts
Council in the production of this book.

Text copyright ©1986 by Jean Little
Illustrations copyright ©1986 by Barbara Di Lella

PRINTED IN CANADA

Typeset by TransCanada Graphics
Book Design by Michael Solomon
Kids Can Press Ltd., Toronto

Kids Can Press Ltd. acknowledges and appreciates the
kind permission of Harper & Row, Publishers Inc. to
reprint the following poems:
"My Own Day" and "About Loving" from *Look Through
My Window*. Copyright ©1970 by Jean Little. "Louisa,
Louisa"; "I Said to the World"; "So I'm Proud";
"Today"; and "Clothes" from *Kate*. Copyright ©1971 by
Jean Little.

86 0 9 8 7 6 5 4 3 2

Contents

My Introduction to Kate 7

Hey World, Here I Am 9

About Loving 10

Today 11

Parsnips 11

Growing Pains 12

Wars 13

Maybe a Fight 14

Not Enough Emilys 16

So I'm Proud 18

About Notebooks 19

Louisa, Louisa 20

Cartwheels 22

Mr. Entwhistle 23

After English Class 26

Surprise 26

Alone 27

He Was So Little 28

Oranges 28

Every So Often 29

Five Dollars 30

When Someone I Love is Hurt 31

About Poems, Sort of 32

Mrs. Buell 34

Susannah and the Daisies 37

Clothes 38

Mother Has a Talk With Me 39

About Feeling Jewish 40

Mosquitoes 41

Writers *42*
I Told You So *43*
Louisa's Liberation *44*
About Old People *45*
Working Parents *46*
Pearls *47*
About a Greek God *48*
About Angels and Age *49*
Smart Remark *50*
Engaged *51*
My Journals *52*
Afternoon in March *53*
About God *54*
My Own Day *56*
Condensed Version *57*
Extinguished *58*
Mrs. Thurstone *59*
Who You Are *62*
Yesterday *64*

For
Emily Blair and Ellen Rudin
with our love

My Introduction to Kate

I first met Kate Bloomfield when she walked into a book I was writing. The book was later published by Harper and Row under the title *Look Through My Window*. It is about a girl called Emily Blair, and when Kate arrived the evening before school began and stood in the shadows on Emily's lawn, I thought she was just another minor character. I also imagined that I had created her and would remain in control of her. I had a lot to learn about Kate.

Since that first meeting, she, with the strong support of my editor Ellen Rudin, made me turn two manuscripts into one novel, with herself anything but a minor character. I so enjoyed writing her poems in *Look Through My Window* that she gave me the privilege of writing down lots more of them as she thought them up. This led to her persuading me to write, at her dictation, the first draft of another book-length manuscript. That took us three days! It was in the first person and she called it *Kate*. Then she left me, except for dropping by to criticize, while I spent a year rewriting it. *Kate* was also published by Harper and Row. You'd think

7

that would satisfy her. Not my Kate! Now she has me aiding and abetting her in having her poems published in this separate volume.

I love Kate, which is why I give in to her so often. Yet the strange thing about our relationship is that, while I know her almost as well as I know myself, she is Emily's friend, not mine, and she lives in a world I write about and watch but cannot enter. I tell myself that her world would not exist if it were not for me. After all, her poems are written down in *my* handwriting. They are written from her point of view but I think up the words. Yet I have this eerie feeling that Kate might have found somebody else to write her poetry down for her if I hadn't been around. I am often asked if the characters in my books are "real." My answer is, "They seem more real, to me, than you are." This is particularly true of Kate.

Some of the poems in this collection appeared earlier in my novels *Look Through My Window* and *Kate*. If you have read them there, you may notice that certain words or phrases have been changed. Kate is a true writer. She revises her work as she matures. Her poems are dashed down as fast as I can write, in the beginning; but afterwards, she and I read them over and polish them. A few turned out to be trash when we reread them. We threw those away. Some we like have had to be omitted because including them would have made the book too long.

Since these poems are a combined effort, Kate and I are sharing equally in dedicating them to the two people whose friendship brought them into being.

Hey World, Here I Am!

I said to the World, "I've arrived.
I, Kate Bloomfield, have come at last."
The World paid no attention.
I said to the World, "Hey World, here I am!
Don't you understand?
It's me, Kate Bloomfield."
The World ignored me.
I took myself off into a corner.
"Guess what?" I whispered. "I made it.
You know...Kate Bloomfield."
My Self bellowed, "YeaaaAAY, Kate!"
And spun six somersaults up the middle of Main Street.
The World turned.
"What did you say?" said the World.
I paid no attention.
After all, I gave it its chance.
It's not my fault that it missed me.

About Loving

In my family, we don't talk much about loving.

My mother never bakes us pies or knits us socks. More than once, she's put cream in my father's coffee, although he takes it black. When she gets home from work she collapses, with her feet up. I have to shake her awake when it's time to eat.

My father never sends her roses or Valentines. He just says to her, "April, listen to this. April!" Then she yawns and opens half an eye and listens, while he reads her something by E.B. White or Tolstoy.

I listen, too. And they listen when I find something so perfect it must be shared. Nobody ever says, "Not now. I'm busy."

But nobody asks me about my homework either. And I do not wait to be told it's time for bed. If I want to floss my teeth, that's my affair. They couldn't care less.

I used to think they didn't know I was there. If I disappeared, I thought, they'd never notice.

But I was wrong.

My father looks up, all at once, and asks me, "Katharine, tell me, what is truth?" And he doesn't go back to his book till he's heard my answer.

My mother does leave me to get the supper ready. But she brings me home ten brand new drawing pencils.

Someday I'll send my mother one dozen roses. Someday I'll knit my father a pair of socks. When I have children I'll tell them, "It's time for bed."

But I'll also ask them sometimes, "What is truth?" And I'll leave them to get the supper and bring them pencils.

Loving isn't as simple as I once thought. Talking about it isn't what matters most.

Today

Today I will not live up to my potential.
Today I will not relate well to my peer group.
Today I will not contribute in class.
    I will not volunteer one thing.
Today I will not strive to do better.
Today I will not achieve or adjust or grow enriched
    or get involved.
I will not put up my hand even if the teacher is wrong
    and I can prove it.

Today I might eat the eraser off my pencil.
I'll look at clouds.
I'll be late.
I don't think I'll wash.

I need a rest.

Parsnips

When I'm home, parsnips make me gag.
    I cannot swallow them.
When I'm out I behave like a lady and, somehow,
    they go down.
Mother says I could eat them at home, if I tried.
She's wrong.

Growing Pains

Mother got mad at me tonight and bawled me out.
She said I was lazy and self-centred.
She said my room was a pigsty.
She said she was sick and tired of forever nagging
    but I gave her no choice.
She went on and on until I began to cry.
I hate crying in front of people. It was horrible.

I got away, though, and went to bed and it was over.
I knew things would be okay in the morning;
Stiff with being sorry, too polite, but okay.
I was glad to be by myself.

Then she came to my room and apologized.
She explained, too.
Things had gone wrong all day at the store.
She hadn't had a letter from my sister
    and she was worried.
Dad had also done something to hurt her.
She even told me about that.
Then *she* cried.
I kept saying, "It's all right. Don't worry."
And wishing she'd stop.

I'm just a kid.
I can forgive her getting mad at me. That's easy.
But her sadness...
I don't know what to do with her sadness.
I yell at her often, "You don't understand me!"
But I don't want to have to understand her.
That's expecting too much.

Wars

When I was in Grade Two, I said to my father,
"I think wars are wrong!
People should be told to stop all this fighting right now.
If I were crowned Queen of the World,
    I'd make wars against the law."
My father said I had something there,
But he didn't seem terribly excited.
I could not understand him.

Then I went upstairs and caught my sister Marilyn
Playing with my new paper dolls without my permission!

We had a war.

Maybe a Fight

Emily and I were about to have a fight. I could feel it in the air, like a thunderstorm coming. I was in a foul mood and she was feeling much the same. It was going to happen any minute.

Yet I didn't feel strong enough to get good and mad and then go to the trouble of making peace. We were going to end up barely speaking for at least two days and we'd both hate it. It's terrible, when you are dying to talk, to have just made a vow never to speak to the other person again.

"Emily Blair," I said, struggling with my conflicting emotions, "are you trying to pick a fight with me?"

"I wasn't, but I *will*, if that's what you're after," she growled.

Then, in the nick of time, my mother walked in. She looked from me to Emily and back again. Then she plugged in the kettle. "What's wrong with you two?" she asked.

We didn't answer. We glowered. By now, we knew we had gone too far to back down. The fight had as good as started.

Mother pulled out a chair and sat down. "Why don't you both just pitch in and start calling each other names?" she said. "If you hurry you can get it out of your systems before the kettle boils. Then we can all have some tea. Kate, you begin."

"Why me?" I yelped, feeling like an idiot.

"Because you are the hostess, of course. Tell her she's... two-faced and bossy and preachy. Go on, Kate. Do I have to dictate your entire part?"

"But she isn't. Not two-faced anyway," I said. "And we're both bossy sometimes...." I ground to a halt.

Emily had started getting out the tea things.

"When I'm preachy, you have it coming," she said, over her shoulder.

The kettle began to sing. Emily poured boiling water into the teapot. She kept her back turned.

All at once, I knew I was going to laugh. No matter how hard I tried not to, I could feel giggles bubbling up inside me. I chuckled. Mother joined in. And when Emily turned around, she was wearing this silly grin.

"Be careful. It's hot," she instructed, handing us each our mug. Then, holding her own aloft, she said, "To us, champion lightweight battlers of Riverside!"

"Don't forget me," my mother said. "I did most of the work." Then she took a swallow, instead of just pretending like Emily, and burned her tongue.

Afterwards I asked Emily, "Did we have a fight or didn't we?"

"Weren't you there?" was all she would answer.

Not Enough Emilys

There are not enough Emilys in the world.
What I mean is ... Emily is the kind of person
  everybody needs to have sometimes.
And suppose I didn't?

Take last Saturday.
When I came to the breakfast table, the kitchen was
  spilling over, bursting with sunshine.
The radio was on and the man said something about
"A cold front moving in from Michigan" and
"Dress warmly, because of the wind chill factor."
But there was this sparkling world of shining sunlight
So I said, "It's spring!"

Mother snapped right back, through her teeth,
"No. You may *not* wear knee socks."

Now knee socks had not once crossed my mind.
After all, I had heard the man on the radio too.
Ignoring her, I sat down.
"Dad," I said to the back of *The Globe and Mail*,
"It's spring."
"Not by the thermometer it isn't," he grunted.

Oh, it was understandable.
I didn't yell at them or anything.
They were making perfect sense.
But who needs sense every minute?

Feeling discouraged, I went over to Emily's.
I just about froze to death on the way there, too!

Her mother opened the door. She's nice.
I thought it couldn't hurt to try.
I waved my mitt at all the shining morning.
"Mrs. Blair," I announced, "it's spring."
"Spring's coming all right," she said, reaching out
  and pulling me inside.
Then, just as I thought 'Hurray!' she went and added,
"In two and a half months, if we're lucky."
She smiled as she said it.
Still...
I dragged my feet on my way up to Emily's room.
I was going to try once more.
Emily's usually with me. But what if she weren't?

The minute she saw me, before I could open my mouth,
"Kate," she said, "guess what!"

I could tell she knew.
"What?" I said and waited, hoping that I was right.
"Spring's here!" Emily said.

It's queer how feelings turn upside-down sometimes.
I didn't even smile. "You nut," I told her,
"It's only the third of February."
I sounded mad.

Emily laughed at me, just sat on her bed and laughed.
Then she said, "Hey, let's have a picnic down by the river.
We could take apples."
"And doughnuts," I said.
"We have some doughnuts left over from last night."

So that's what we did — and it was so cold
Our hands and feet went numb and I thought we'd perish...

And yet
The sun made the morning glisten and shout for joy
And we laughed a lot — and it was great to be us.

And that's what I mean about Emily.

Since then, when we were taking world problems in school
(Refugees, inflation, terrorism, famine, race riots
And the threat of Nuclear War),
And the teacher started that stuff about it being
Our "responsibility to change things," to make better laws ...
As though our class could fix the whole big mess,
It came to me, suddenly, that maybe the world needs
Not only better laws — but more Emilys.

Everybody should be able to walk to a river.
Everybody should sometimes decide "It's spring!"
Everybody should have an apple to take.
But mostly, everybody should have a friend.

So I'm Proud

Our History teacher says, "Be proud you're Canadians."
My father says, "You can be proud you're Jewish."
My mother says, "Stand up straight, Kate.
    Be proud you're tall."

So I'm proud.

But what I want to know is,
When did I have the chance to be
    Norwegian or Buddhist or short?

About Notebooks

I love the first page of a new notebook.
I write the date crisply.
My whole name marches exactly along the line.
The spaces are always even.
The commas curl just so.
I never have to erase on the first page.
Never!

When I get to the middle, there are lots of eraser holes.
The corners are dog-eared.
Whole paragraphs have been crossed out.
My words slide off the lines and crowd together.
I wish it was done.

I have a dream that, someday, someone will say,
"Here, give me that beat-up old notebook.
You needn't bother filling in all those other zillion pages.
Start a new one this instant
— Because it's February, because today's not Wednesday,
Because everybody deserves beginning again more often."

Yet, crazy as it sounds,
I always like to write the number 8,
Even on the third last page of a messy notebook.
It meets itself so neatly it's almost magic.
And I love swooping big E's and looping small z's.
If, for some reason, I get to write a word
Like "quintessence" maybe or something with lots of m's
Or "balloon" or "rainbow" or "typhoon" or "lollipop"
I forget I'm sick of the book with its stupid margins
And, while I'm writing, I hum inside my head.

Louisa, Louisa

My family is having dinner with the Blairs.
I come early.
Emily shows off her sister Louisa.
Louisa, being only six weeks old, is not interested.
She keeps falling asleep.

"Smile, Louisa," Emily orders, joggling her.
"Smile for Kate."
Louisa yawns,
Waves one fist haphazardly and firmly closes both eyes.

"Emily, come and help me put the leaf in the table,"
  Mrs. Blair calls.
"Drat!" says Emily. She hands over the baby.
"Hold her," she commands, and disappears.

So I hold you, Louisa.
I sit very still and
I hold you and watch you sleep.
For a moment, you are all mine.
Not that there is much of you...
But your eyelids flutter...I can feel you breathing...
You are terribly alive, Louisa.
There is so much you do not know.
Louisa, you do not know about school!
Do you know words yet, Louisa? No, no words.
You have never heard of dying, Louisa.

...Shhh...sleep...

You will discover the sun.
You will see Emily laughing.

You will come upon the alphabet and rainbows.
You will ride an escalator.
You will read *The Secret Garden* for the first time.
You may love a boy called…Arthur. Or Bill.
You may go to Africa.
You'll get a letter.
You will wear shoes and create a dance all your own.

Here is a secret, Louisa.
Living is worth schools.
Loving balances computers.
Even dying, Louisa, and knowing about dying,
    cannot stop your dancing.

But now I am holding you
And you are sleeping.
Louisa, shh.
I love you right now, Louisa, before you know anything,
Before you even know that you are Louisa.

Cartwheels

I can't turn cartweels. I've tried and tried.
I can start. I can get about halfway...
Then I buckle over somehow and collapse sideways.

I told Mother. "Practise," she advised.
I said I had. It didn't work. I just plain couldn't do them.

"Well, you can write poems," she said,
"And you're so good at Math..."
She went on and on and it was all very nice.
I appreciated it.

I still can't turn cartwheels.

Mr. Entwhistle

Mr. Entwhistle was our supply teacher. He had big shoulders and a mean mouth. He knew, before he'd laid eyes on us, that we were out to make trouble. And he knew how to handle teenagers. Step on them hard, right from the start, and you'd have no discipline problems. He'd show us who was boss the first time one of us stepped out of line.

Looking back, I can see that was how it started. But at the time, I had not gotten around to noticing him, except to see that he was young. That's a nice change, I thought, and went back to attempting to show Sandra Mayhew where she'd fouled up in the Math homework.

Mr. Entwhistle had started writing our names in on a seating plan. He knew all the tricks. He wasn't going to put up with desk jumpers.

"What's your name?" he asked sharply.

I didn't look up, let alone answer. Sandra was finally catching on. It never once crossed my mind that he was speaking to me.

"I said '*What is your name?*'" he blasted, making a real production out of it. He was closer to me. He had started down our aisle. So I glanced up. I still had not realized that I was the one he was addressing. I sat there, gazing at him, wondering why he was all charged up. I did not tell him my name.

"All right. That does it!" he thundered. "You can go to the Office."

"Me?" I said in blank amazement.

I was bewildered. Yet he was glaring straight at me. His eyes were greenish with brown speckles. They seemed to be on the point of falling out. He was absolutely frantic.

"Yes, you. Oh, yes indeed, you! Perhaps next time you'll show respect," he babbled, side-stepping to his desk like a giant crab and scribbling a note for me to take. I couldn't see

23

what he wrote but Pete Evans told me later that it was something about insubordination. I did see that his hand was shaking. I sat there, stunned. I honestly believed that, any minute now, I'd wake up.

"On your feet!" Mr. Entwhistle shrieked. Maybe it only sounded like a shriek to me. But his voice did seem to get louder every time he spoke.

I stood up slowly. Outside the open window, the sun was shining. Everything was green, beguiling. "Come," it said to me. "Just come out and away." I considered it.

At the selfsame instant, some other part of me shouted, as angrily as Mr. Entwhistle could have done, "Fight back, Kate. The bell hasn't gone. You have your rights. The others will back you up. Fight!"

Then our eyes met and I saw that he was afraid. He was just a person. He had made a mistake and now, too late, he knew it. He'd rage and bluster if I stood up to him. He'd have to. All the same, he was wishing he could go back and start over. I've felt like that.

"Yes, sir," I said quietly, and reached out my hand for the note. Nobody moved. Nobody breathed even. I was waiting for him to hand it to me; the rest of the kids, maybe, for me to start an argument. I often do. Mr. Entwhistle... who knows?

Then it was as though someone said, "Will the real Mr. Entwhistle please stand up?" The bombast went out of him. For one more moment, he hesitated.

"Never mind," he blurted then. "Sit down. We'll let it pass this time."

He tore the note in half, crumpled it up, and threw it at the wastebasket. Even though he missed and the wad of paper landed on the floor, even though I'd won in some way, and he'd had to back down, he looked taller.

Taking my seat I felt a bit taller myself. I shoved my hands out of sight when I saw that they were trembling. Sunlight flooded the room.

"Way to go, Kate!" Sandra cheered in a too-loud whisper.
I scowled at her.
"Shh," I said.

After English Class

I used to like "Stopping by Woods on a Snowy Evening."
I liked the coming darkness,
The jingle of harness bells, breaking — and adding to
   — the stillness,
The gentle drift of snow....

But today, the teacher told us what everything stood for.
The woods, the horse, the miles to go, the sleep —
They all have 'hidden meanings.'

It's grown so complicated now that,
Next time I drive by,
I don't think I'll bother to stop.

Surprise

I feel like the ground in winter,
Hard, cold, dark, dead, unyielding.

Then hope pokes through me
Like a crocus.

Alone

I am alone ... and lonely.

My own sadness makes everything around me
    more beautiful.
The dusk falls softly,
As simply as a page turning or a bird lighting on the ground.
The sky grows dull rose near the rooftops
And, high above me, a sea-blue-green.
I am caught up in it all — and small.
I search for words. I ache with words I cannot find.

Inside, the phone rings.
"Where's Kate?" Dad asks.

I am here — but I say nothing.
He calls — but I do not answer.

"She's not in yet," he says to someone.
"I'll tell her you phoned."

I could go in.

Soon it will be suppertime anyway,
Time for eating and talking and being part of things,
Belonging again to the horrible, boring, nice, funny,
    noisy, busy, angry, loving world of people.

I'll go in when I have to.
In half an hour, I'll even like it.

Now...
Now I'll stay out here, hugging my separateness,
    my oneness.

I am alone. I am lonely.
I am growing into me.

He Was So Little

He was so little he had to sit on a book
To be tall enough to reach his spoon and fork.
Yet, when his mother began to put on his bib,
He pushed it away. "I'm not a baby," he snapped.
And he sat very straight and tried to look adult.

"How are you getting along?" my father asked.
"Would you like me to spread your bread?"
"No, thank you," he replied. "I prefer it bare."

It wasn't really funny, not funny at all.
He looked bewildered and wounded when they all laughed.

I wanted to make them stop, to scream at them,
"Can't you remember what it was like to be small?
Didn't you ever, ever make a mistake?"
I wanted to shout, but I did not speak one word.

And, as their laughter died and his hot cheeks cooled,
I looked at myself and caught the smile on my face.
It's queer sometimes, being this age I am.
It's like being out on a battlefield in a war
— But never being quite sure whose side you're on.

Oranges

I peel oranges neatly.
The sections come apart cleanly, perfectly, in my hands.

When Emily peels an orange, she tears holes in it.
Juice squirts in all directions.

"Kate," she says, "I don't know how you do it!"

Emily is my best friend.
I hope she never learns how to peel oranges.

Every So Often

Every so often, my father tries making bread.
He's too impatient though.
He puts it on top of the radiator to make it rise faster
And I doubt if he kneads it as long as the books
    say he should.
He likes to see results.
When it's baking, the whole house smells like heaven.
But you do have to hurry and eat it while it's fresh.
The next day, it's almost too heavy to lift.

The mood only strikes him once every couple of years.
Mother shakes her head and gets out of his way.
But I sit around and cheer him on. It's exciting!

I've no idea what starts him off on bread-making.
But I'm glad he does it.
It makes him ridiculous, mysterious
    and my own particular father.

Five Dollars

A long time ago, last August or September, I took a five dollar bill from Mother's purse. I even forget, now, what I needed it for. She was sleeping and I didn't want to bother her. I think I had to pay a fine at the Library and pick up some shoes that had been repaired. I really don't know.

I was going to tell her, though, as soon as I got back, but I forgot. And she never missed it. When I did remember, she was at work. I kept forgetting — and remembering again, always at the wrong time.

In bed at night, I'd think of it, or in school, right in the middle of History. The absolutely crazy part of it is, she wouldn't have minded. Not back then. But, by now, it's been too long. By now, if I told her, it would be like confessing. By now, I feel as though I stole it. I didn't though. I'll tell her. I'll just casually tell her. (I can't. I've tried.)

I'll have to put five dollars back some time when she has enough money she won't notice. But five dollars! There are always so many places to spend five dollars.

I'll tell her tonight. She'll understand. It's nothing really. We'll both laugh about it once it's done. Oh, I wish it was over!

When Someone I Love Is Hurt

When someone I love is hurt,
I never know what to say.
I scowl and growl.
I slam doors.
I shut myself up in my room and put KEEP OUT on the door.
I glare at people who say things like,
"You certainly got out of bed on the wrong side
  this morning!"
I can't even run away into my favourite books.
The hurting follows me there and won't let me stay.
I just lie on my bed and concentrate on not crying.
I am not one tiny bit helpful.
I act dumb with everybody,
Even people who are completely outside it all,
Like the paper boy or Emily's aunt.
Even when I know I'm being stupid
  and only making things worse,
I can't help it.

But, all the time, I'm hurting too.
I yearn, with every atom of me, to make things right
  for the person I love.

It would be better to be comforting,
To be cheery, to make little jokes,
Or even just to say how sorry I am.

I can't. Hardly ever.
I just ache and ache and ache.

About Poems, Sort of

I wrote a poem about Emily and spring — and it was right.
Exactly what I meant was there on the page.
I read it to Mother. Her face lighted.
"Oh Kate," she said, "I do like that."

Shyly, happily, I turned to go away.
Then I turned back.
"Haven't you ever written a poem?" I asked her.

She shook her head.
"Not one," she said calmly.

"How can you stand it...
I mean, never, ever making a special thing all your own..."
I stared at her.
I felt as though we were two entirely different
    kinds of beings.

She smiled at me.
Her face looked...I don't know...unguarded.
"I've had you, Kate," she said.
"I've worked over you and you're special
And my own."

We were both embarrassed.
I was surprised, too, and disbelieving.
I stood, tongue-tied, my cheeks reddening.
I wasn't going to say anything.
Then, the words jumped out of my mouth, bang!

"I thought you didn't want me.
You didn't either. I've even heard you say so myself."

Her eyes went wide.
All at once, she laughed.
"Oh, *how* I didn't want you!" she admitted.

"I was so mad.
But when I think of life without you...
I did want you, Kate.
I didn't know it right away, that's all.
Be reasonable.
How was I to guess, ahead of time, that *you* were the one
    who was coming...
Have you brushed your teeth?"

She hasn't asked me that for years.
She usually forgot even when I was little.

"No," I said.

I had to clear my throat before I spoke.

"Then go brush them," she ordered.

So I went.
But it was almost as though I'd written another poem.

Or she had.

Mrs. Buell

For years and years, for what seems like forever, I've gone to BUELLS when I had a dime to spare. It's a run-down, not very clean, corner store. Kids go there mostly, for licorice and bubble gum and jawbreakers and popsicles and comic books and cones. She only has three flavours and the cones taste stale. Still, she'll sell you one scoop for fifteen cents. It's not a full scoop but it's cheaper than anywhere else. It's the only place I know where a kid can spend one penny.

Mrs. Buell is run-down too, and a grouch. She never smiles or asks you how you are. Little kids are scared to go in there alone. We laugh at them but really, we understand. We felt it too, when we were smaller and had to face her towering behind the counter.

She was always the same except that once. I tripped going in, and fell and scraped my knee. It hurt so much that I couldn't move for a second. I was winded too, and I had to gasp for breath. I managed not to cry out but I couldn't keep back the tears.

Mrs. Buell is big but she moved like lightning. She hauled a battered wooden chair out from behind the curtain that hung across the back. Then, without a word, she picked me up and sat me down on it. We were alone in the store but I wasn't afraid. Her hands, scooping me up, had been work-roughened; hard but kind.

She still didn't speak. Instead, she took a bit of rag out of her sweater pocket, bent down and wiped the smear of blood off my knee. The rag looked greyish but her hands were gentle. I think she liked doing it. Then she fetched a Band-Aid and stuck it on.

"Does it still sting?" she asked, speaking at last, in a voice I'd never heard her use before.

I shook my head. And she smiled. At least I think she did. It only lasted a fraction of a second. And I wasn't looking straight at her.

At that moment Johnny Tresano came in with one nickel clutched in his fist. He was so intent on the candies he hardly noticed me. He stood and stood, trying to decide.

"Make up your mind or take yourself off," she growled.

She had gone back behind the counter. I waited for her to look at me again so that I could thank her. But when he left she turned her back and began moving things around on the shelves. I had meant to buy some jujubes but I lost my nerve. After all, everybody knew she hated kids. She was probably sorry now that she'd fixed my knee. I slunk out without once opening my mouth.

Yet, whenever I looked down and saw the Band-Aid, I felt guilty. As soon as one corner came loose, I pulled it off and threw it away. I didn't go near the store for weeks.

She was terribly fat. She got so hot in summer that her hair hung down in wet strings and her clothes looked limp. In winter she wore the same sweater every day, a man's grey one, too big, with the sleeves pushed up. They kept slipping down and she'd shove them back a million times a day. Yet she never rolled up the cuffs to make them shorter.

She never took days off. She was always there. We didn't like her or hate her. We sort of knew that selling stuff to kids for a trickle of small change wasn't a job anybody would choose — especially in that poky little place with flies in summer and the door being opened all winter, letting in blasts of cold air. Even after that day when she fixed my knee, I didn't once wonder about her life.

Then I stopped at BUELLS one afternoon and she wasn't there. Instead, a man and woman I'd never laid eyes on were behind the counter sorting through stacks of stuff. They were getting some boxes down off a high shelf right then so they didn't hear me come in. I was so amazed I just stood there gawking.

"How Ma stood this cruddy hole I'll never know!" the woman said, backing away from a cloud of dust. "Didn't she ever clean?"

"Give the subject a rest, Glo," he answered. "She's dead. She won't bother you any longer."

"I tried, Harry. You know I tried. Over and over, I told her she could move in with us. God knows I could have used a bit of cash and her help looking after those kids."

I think I must have made a sound then. Anyway, she whirled around and saw me.

"This place is closed," she snapped. "Harry, I thought I told you to lock the door. What did you want?"

I didn't want anything from her. But I still could not believe Mrs. Buell wasn't there. I stared around.

"I said we're shut. If you don't want anything, beat it," she told me.

The minute I got home I phoned Emily. She said her mother had just read it in the paper.

"She had a daughter!" Emily said, her voice echoing my own sense of shock. "She died of a heart attack. Kate, her whole name was Katharine Ann Buell."

"Katharine," I said slowly. My name is really Katharine although only Dad calls me by it. "I can't believe it somehow."

"No," Emily said. "She was always just Mrs. Buell."

I told her about Glo and Harry. After we hung up though, I tried to imagine Mrs. Buell as a child. Instead, I saw her bending down putting that Band-Aid on my knee. Her hair had been thin on top, I remembered, and she'd had dandruff. She had tried not to hurt me. Glo's voice, talking about her, had been so cold. Had she had anyone who loved her? It seemed unlikely. Why hadn't I smiled back?

But, to be honest, something else bothered me even more. Her going had left a hole in my life. Because of it I knew, for the first time, that nothing was safe — not even the everyday, taken for granted, background of my being. Like Mrs. Buell, pushing up her sweater sleeves and giving me my change.

Susannah and the Daisies

I saw Susannah going slowly around the lawn,
Checking daisy after daisy with intense concentration,
But not picking any.

"What *are* you doing?" I finally asked.

"I'm trying to find one that'll end up at
   'He loves me' before I pick it.
They're too pretty to pick by mistake," she said.

I went to help. It's trickier than you'd think.
It's hard to remember which petal you started with.

When she had one, I watched her solemnly
   take off the petals, one by one.
"He loves me...he loves me not...he loves me!"

"Who loves you?" I teased.

"My brother Marcus," she said.

Clothes

I like new clothes.
They seem brighter, smoother, shinier.
I move carefully in them.
I remember to hang them up.
I feel taller in them — and prettier —
And I don't climb over barbed wire fences.

I like old clothes too.
I don't think about them much.
They are part of me,
Going where I go, doing whatever I feel like doing.
They are less bother and more comfortable.
They don't expect me to be so tall;
They know my size exactly.

You know, it's a funny thing...
Friends are like clothes.

Mother Has a Talk With Me

"I want to have a talk with you, Katharine," my mother said.
She never "has talks" with me
   and she doesn't call me Katharine.
"Yes?" I said, on guard, intrigued.
"I've been told that you've been seeing a lot
   of that Nelson boy," she said.
She sounded slightly nervous. I wanted to laugh.
I only wished the rumour were true.
But I said coolly, "I don't like some of your friends
But I don't consider it my business to mention it."
"Your sudden disappearances speak volumes," Mother said,
   relaxing,
"And your trapped look when you haven't made
   your getaway in time."
I laughed and told her the truth.
"I really like Dave Nelson. So does every other girl in school.
But he hardly knows I'm alive."

Mother gave me a long, thoughtful look.
"Maybe we should see about having your hair
   properly styled," she said.
My mouth dropped open.
"Well," Mother said, going pink,
"I don't want you conspicuous but
I don't want you invisible either, Kate!"

I went to bed confused — but mostly amused at Mother.

About Feeling Jewish

I wanted to feel Jewish. I didn't know how. I told Emily.

"You mean, you don't?" Emily said, with interest.

I looked at a spot over her head and almost wished I hadn't told her. "Not really," I muttered. "At least...I don't think I do."

Emily gave it serious thought. And I knew telling her had been right, after all. That's one of my favourite things about Emily. She hardly ever laughs when she shouldn't.

"Read some books," she advised, at last. "Maybe that would help. It's somewhere to start, anyway."

I had already dipped into a couple, but this time, I sat myself down and read properly. I struggled through over half a book called *Judaism*. I read almost all of a book called *What is a Jew?* (The only thing he left out was the answer.) I read big chunks of a fat book called *Jews, God and History*. And I read every word of Rabbi Plaut's book *Your Neighbour is a Jew*. I thought, what with him being a Canadian, it might help more than the others. I learned millions of things, both fascinating and dull. I still didn't feel Jewish.

"It didn't work," I reported to Emily.

"Well," she said, helplessly, "you wait. Something will."

Nearly a month went by. Then I read *The Diary of Anne Frank* and I read *The Endless Steppe*.

"Hey, guess what?" I burst out, when I got Emily by herself. "I read these books — and it happened! I feel Jewish!"

Emily grinned. "Good," she said. She borrowed both books. Emily and I swap books all the time. Two days later, she brought them back.

"Kate," she said, as she handed them to me, "brace yourself."

"What for?"

"They made me feel Jewish too," Emily said.

Mosquitoes

I came in just in time for supper
But there wasn't any.
Mother was lying on the couch with her eyes shut.
"Mother," I said, "what are you doing?"
I thought she wasn't going to answer.
She didn't open her eyes.
But, after a minute, she said,
"Use your powers of observation, Kate.
Obviously I am leading the animals into the Ark
    — two by two."
"What do you want for supper?" I asked.
…Silence…
"Mother," I began again.
"Don't interrupt me," she murmured from far away,
"Or I might forget mosquitoes."

So I made Kraft dinner and a salad.
When I took her plate in to her, she had fallen asleep.
She comes home from work terribly tired some nights.
I put her macaroni in the oven and her salad in the
    refrigerator.
Then, right in the middle of doing French, I thought,
"Maybe we won't have any mosquitoes this summer."
I laughed out loud and wakened her.
"What's so funny?" she yawned.
"Never mind," I said. I got her her supper.
She didn't make me explain.
Maybe she knew
That saying one word more would have spoiled it.

Writers

Emily writes of poetic things
Like crocuses and hummingbirds' wings,
But I think people beat hummingbirds every time.

Emily likes to write of snow
And dawn and candlelight aglow,
But I'd rather write about me and Emily and stuff like that.

The funny thing is, I delight
To read what Emily likes to write,
And Emily says she thinks my poems are okay too.

Also, sometimes, we switch with each other.
Emily writes of a fight with her mother.
I tell about walking alone by the river,
     — how still and golden it was.

I know what Emily means, you see,
And, often, Emily's halfway me...
Oh, there's just no way to make anybody else understand.

We're not a bit the same and yet,
We're closer than most people get.
There's no one word for it. We just care about each other
     the way we are supposed to.

So I can look through Emily's eyes
And she through mine. It's no surprise,
When you come right down to it, that we're friends.

I Told You So

My mother never says, "I told you so."
She doesn't believe in it.
She calls it "rubbing salt in the wound."
But sometimes, her silences are so loud
That we wish she'd give in, for once,
And get it off our minds.

Louisa's Liberation

Emily and I got talking and we decided
It was up to us to make sure Louisa grew up liberated.
"They start teaching them sex-stereotypes
    in Nursery School, my mother read," I said.
"Well, there's no time like the present," said Emily.
"Let's find her and *do* something."

We went in search of Louisa.
She was in the backyard with all her toys laid out in a row.
She was trundling around, as busy as a bee,
    so involved she didn't even notice us arriving.

"Louisa, what are you doing?" Emily asked.
Louisa, still preoccupied, answered, "This is my hospital.
These need operations. Those are dying."

Emily and I exchanged looks as Louisa went back to work.
"Isn't that great!" murmured Emily.
"She's not stuck in a kitchen, playing house; she's a nurse!"

Louisa glanced up.
"No, I'm not," she said. "I'm a doctor."

About Old People

It all started when I told Emily that I didn't like old people.
Well, I don't. They scare me — especially the really ancient
  ones.
I never know what to say to them.
They stare as if you had dirt on your face.
They grab at you, and their hands are hard and bony.
They always want to kiss you. I hate their prickly kisses.
"She's got her father's ears," they say.
As if you're made out of used parts.
Sometimes they smell musty. Often they're nosy.
And you have to be polite, no matter how rude they are.
As I said, I don't like them.

When I said so to Emily, though, she was stunned!
You'd think I'd said I hated newborn babies or kittens.
"But you like Mrs. Thurstone, don't you?" she said at last.

I hadn't been thinking of Mrs. Thurstone.
She used to live next door to the Blairs, before they moved.
She's old all right. Eighty-six is no spring chicken.
"Sure," I said, laughing.
Just thinking about Mrs. Thurstone makes me laugh.
She's so fierce and scary, and then she hands you a present.
I could see what Emily was getting at, of course.

"But she's somebody we know.
I meant I don't like old people in general."

Emily let that sink in.
I thought we'd finished with the topic.
Then she said, all in a rush,
"You know, Kate, every old person in general
  is somebody...
Somebody in particular."

I blinked.
"What?" I said.
Emily took a deep breath and tried again.
"Every old person is somebody," she said.

That was when her cousin James butted in.
I haven't a clue where he sprang from or how much
    he'd heard.
All at once he was there, though, and he snorted,
"You dope, Emily, everybody is somebody.
Not just old people."

We laughed at him.
Then Emily said sternly, "Don't interrupt, James.
Can't you see we're having a serious discussion?"

He took off and we went on to something else.

But, later, I got to thinking.
"Everybody is somebody," James had said.

He's only nine but he's somebody, that's for sure.
So's Emily and so's Mrs. Thurstone.
And I know I'm somebody.
And...old people?

Working Parents

I've read lots of articles about working mothers.
I have a working mother.
I also have a working father
— And I think he deserves mention!

Pearls

Dad gave me a string of pearls for my birthday.
They aren't real pearls but they look real.
They came nested in deep, deep blue velvet
   in a hinged box with a silvery lid.
His sister had some like them when she was my age.
She was thrilled.
He thought I'd really like them.
I said I did.

I love the box.

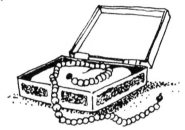

About a Greek God

"Dominic Tantardini looks like a Greek god," I said to the others.

"Would you believe Italian?" Emily asked.

"Italian... Greek... What does it matter? Divine is divine," I told her.

"He has pimples all over his forehead. That's why he wears his hair in his eyes," said Emily.

"I like John Hollingsforth better," Lindsay put in dreamily. But we ignored her.

"Emily Blair, you are no poet!" I accused.

"Katharine Bloomfield, you are no... realist," she laughed back.

I took a deep breath and prepared to demolish her. Before I could, she added, "I do know what you mean, though. He's... he's..."

"Like a Greek god?" I suggested.

"Well... in a far, far distant way, yes," Emily said.

"He phoned me last night," Lindsay remarked, so lightly, so casually, so... *oooooogh*!

"Who?" we demanded, glaring already, knowing full well.

"Nick. He wants me to help him with his homework. I told him I hadn't time."

Lin did look sheepish, I'll say that for her. Emily and I bent double, laughing. It takes the two of us to keep her passing respectably. She's not stupid exactly; she's just lazy about thinking. She also has no feeling for divinity.

Nick: she'll be calling him Nicky next. I'd hit her — except I'd never be able to explain why. And, when you come right down to it, at this point in my life I'm not ready to trade in an old friend on a new Greek god — especially when the Greek god doesn't know I'm alive!

We studied Irony last week in English. I guess this is it. I'm *so* good at homework.

About Angels and Age

This morning, I saw Susan Rosenthal standing in the snow,
   in the Blairs' front yard.
"What are you doing here, Susannah?" I asked,
   smiling at her.
"I'm baby-sitting Louisa," she answered,
   looking responsible.
I felt old.

Louisa, bundled to the eyes in snowsuit, mittens,
   scarf and boots, and completely covered with snow,
   sat up and became visible.
"She showed me how to make angels," she said,
   all excitement.
"Did you ever do that in the olden days, Kate?"

I knew I had on the wrong clothes, but I did not feel
   that old.
"Just watch me," I told her and did three perfect ones.
I also got soaked to the skin.

"What on earth have you been doing?" Mother asked
   when I came dripping home.

"Being angelic," I told her.

Smart Remark

When my older sister Marilyn came for a visit,
She spent most of her time trying to make us over
Into some other kind of family.
The kind you see on TV who get all excited and beam
Because they're having Lipton's Chicken Noodle soup
   for supper.
The kind who pick to spend the whole day in the new Mall.
The kind who love to do things together and talk non-stop.
The kind we aren't.

When she said, for the fifteenth time,
"Kate, must you always have your head in a book?"
The worm turned and I snapped, "Yes. I must.
It's better than having no head
— Like you!"

Dad laughed.
Mother sent me to my room.

Afterwards, she said,
"It was clever, Kate. It may even have been true.
But you didn't have to hurt her."

"She hurt *me*!" I complained.
"Did she really?" Mother asked, looking me in the eye.
"Oh, I guess not," I said, thinking back over the visit.
"But she drove me crazy, picking at me...and..."

"You wanted to swat her," Mother finished for me.
"So did we all. But you don't swat butterflies, Kate."
"If she's a butterfly, what am I?" I demanded.
"A mosquito," my father joined in.
"But Marilyn's not exactly a butterfly, April.
She's more like a...tent caterpillar."

Mother laughed.
Why didn't she send *him* to his room?

I know why.
He said it when Marilyn couldn't hear.
In other words, behind her back.
Which makes him a spider?

And Mother...a...a...
Queen Bee, I suppose.

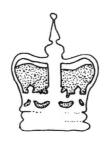

Engaged

My parents have never told Marilyn and me
How they got engaged or exactly where or when.
We've asked over and over.
They look at each other and laugh.
"Wasn't it in that restaurant," Mother says,
    "where the gypsy played?"
"Oh, no, no! On the steamship behind the lifeboat,"
    Dad reminds her.
Then they laugh again. They make Marilyn furious.
But I like wondering
— And I like the way they laugh together,
    leaving us both outside.

My Journals

Real writers keep journals. I've had four.

When Mother told my sister Marilyn that I loved to write, she sent me a journal for my birthday. It was squarish and fat, with small, organized pages. It had a shiny pink cover with MY DIARY written on it in scrolled, gold letters. A flimsy padlock, which would break if you looked at it, was supposed to keep it secret. Every page had two skimpy sections, with a date at the top of each. There was space enough for maybe three sentences if your handwriting was small. My handwriting scrawls. Besides, my life is too big to fit into those squinched-up pages. I gave it to my friend Lindsay Ross. She adores it. She has a smaller life. And tidy writing.

Then our teacher handed out "journals" which we had to write in every day for one month. She said she wouldn't mark them but she would read them over. I did it and, as assignments go, it wasn't bad. But, of course, you could only put down stuff that you wouldn't mind her knowing. My private life is not her affair. When I got it back, though, and saw she had written *Excellent*! on it, I felt like a fraud.

Then Dad gave me a journal. It is elegant. The pages are creamy and feel like the best art paper when you stroke them. The outside is covered with a deep blue fabric which has tiny nosegays scattered over it. I love it. Maybe, someday, my life will be elegant enough to match it. I hope so. I'm saving it carefully just in case.

My fourth journal I bought for myself. It is a hard cover book meant for writing lecture notes in. It has lots of room on every page. Some days, I write six or seven full pages about what I am feeling and thinking. Or about Emily or school. Other days I don't even pick it up or, if I do, I just write something like "Another day lived through!" I draw pictures in it now and then or paste in a copy of a poem I like.

Getting a journal is like buying shoes. You have to find the one that fits. And you are the only person who can tell if it pinches.

Afternoon in March

I run
Not to anywhere,
Not away from anybody.
I run just to run,
To make my heart wham,
My eyes blur,
My side pain sharply.

I slow down at last,
Gulping the sweet air,
Almost crying...

I'm crazy.

But there was nobody ahead of me
Down that whole, long, waiting stretch of
    sun-bare sidewalk!

Oh, it was like a bird flying,
Like a song,
Like a shout!

I was freedom.

About God

When people talk at me about God, I usually listen.
It's the easiest thing to do and it's polite.
There's also always the chance I might learn something,
But, so far, it's mostly been just a list of names.

I know about God, the Lord, my refuge and my strength,
Jehovah, Yahweh, and the Holy Spirit,
Our-Father-Which-Art-In-Heaven-
   Hallowed-Be-Thy-Name,
The one that's always blessing you when you sneeze,
God in a cloud, God on a throne and God in a burning bush.
I've heard him called a Shepherd — and a Lamb.
He walked in the Garden of Eden, but nobody's seen Him.
He lives in Heaven. He saves you from your sins.
No, no, He's here in us. He's really a spirit.
Or is He Love? Or is He a still, small voice?

Whatever else they say, they insist He's One
(Or three in One?). But He sounds like a crowd to me.
Whoever He is, we have nothing to do with each other.
I've never met Him. I don't think He's around
The places where I hang out. Or, if He is,
He never speaks.

But...sometimes, when I'm afraid, I guess I pray.
I gasp, "Don't let it get me!" or "Please, help me. Please!"
It isn't a thing I plan. The words just come.
And I am braver.
Not every time. Not so it's something sure.
But often enough for me to wonder why...or who...

And when I see somebody hurt — and I can't help —
A father downtown slapping his little boy,
Those people who haunt the News with starving eyes,
Children wounded or lost... and nobody, nobody listens!...
I feel an anger greater than my anger.
I know a pity that is outside myself,
A pity that never turns away and forgets.
I rest in a sorrow too deep to understand.
This might be God. I think I hope it is.

And there are moments when I see something lovely
— Just sunlight, maybe, lying along the road —
And nobody's there to tell, but someone sees.

And the moments when I think up a private joke,
Too silly to say aloud or too all my own...
There's always somebody there to share it with.
Maybe it's only myself. It might be God.

Whether you're God or not, I'm glad
    you're there.
I couldn't call you Thou or He
But then, I think you're tired of
    that jumble of Holy Names
And I'm certain you don't waste
    time on thrones or sneezes.

My Own Day

When I opened my eyes this morning,
The day belonged to me.
The sky was mine and the sun,
And my feet got up dancing.
The marmalade was mine and the squares of sidewalk
And all the birds in the trees.
So I stood and I considered
Stopping the world right there,
Making today go on and on forever.
But I decided not to.
I let the world spin on and I went to school.
I almost did it, but then, I said to myself,
"Who knows what you might be missing tomorrow?"

Condensed Version

When I went over to the Blairs',
Emily was reading her cousin Ann a condensed version
 of *Heidi*.
It was all wrong — the pictures, the words,
 what happened, the way it felt.
"You shouldn't read her that," I said.
"Why not?" asked Emily.
Suddenly, I knew exactly how to explain.
"People who read condensed versions instead of
 the real book," I said loftily,
"Are like people who read a road map
 — and think they've been on a journey."
Emily looked at me, for a moment.
Then she put down the book and clapped.

"*Read*, Emily!" Ann said.

"Let's read *Winnie the Pooh* instead," said Emily.

I stayed to listen.
It was the one about Eeyore's birthday.
We liked it as much as Ann.

How perfect of Emily to clap like that!

Extinguished

I was hating her hotly, fiercely,
When she sighed.
It wasn't one of those sighs you do on purpose,
Exasperated or martyred or Oh-so-patient!
She just sounded tired.
If she'd meant to do it, I could have ignored it with ease.
This way
It worked like the candle-snuffer
   we got her for her birthday.

Mrs. Thurstone

Mrs. Thurstone is in the hospital. She lives alone in the huge stone house next door to the Blairs' old place. She's ninety, and Mother says she may not get better.

"If sheer gumption can do it," Emily's father said, "she'll be out in a week." But everyone's worried.

For all she looks like a witch, Mrs. Thurstone's special. She gives you a present and scolds you when you thank her. She loves watching baseball on TV. She taught Emily and me to play bezique. She corrects my grammar.

I went in to see her yesterday, after school. She didn't know me.

"Mama should never have let you get your hair cut, Nellie," she said. "It looked so lovely long."

I didn't say "Who's Nellie? My name is Kate."

"It'll grow again. My hair grows very fast," I told her.

I pulled up the visitor's chair and I took her hand. Then, all at once, she fell asleep. She lay, looking smaller, breathing through her mouth. Her eyelids seemed almost transparent. I just sat there, watching over her, holding her hand. Usually it is hard for me to sit still. When I was little, Mother called me Fidget. But right then, I didn't want to move. I felt somehow part of her. I even breathed in time with her breathing, except hers was sometimes unsteady.

There were two other old ladies who shared that room. One was gushy, when she was not gabbing on the phone. I was glad she was down in the lounge. The other was unconscious, I guess. She was all hooked up to tubes and she never opened her eyes. Once in a while, she moaned. She had made me nervous at first, but by then I'd grown used to her. She just made me sad.

Mrs. Thurstone opened her eyes. "Kate," she said, as though she'd not been asleep at all, as though she'd never called me Nellie, "I've lived too long."

"You have not. That isn't true," I cried.

"Hush, child. Don't carry on so over nothing," she said, her voice tart and normal. "It's only sometimes I feel that way. Life still has good moments, such as when a young thing like you comes to see me, smelling of fresh air and the whole living world out there."

She glanced over at the other bed and lowered her voice, as if Miss Potts might hear.

"Is it snowing?" she asked me. "I wish I had a bed by the window. I've always loved looking at new snow."

She had been in that bed for almost a month. It will soon be Christmas. I nodded in answer to her question but I began to cry too. I couldn't help it. What if she never...? Maybe she read my mind. She glared at me, fierce as an eagle.

"Hoity toity," she scoffed. "If there is one thing I cannot abide...one thing I....You say it is snowing?"

I could see her forgetting again. I could see her knowing she was forgetting but not mentioning it. She held onto my hand a little tighter. Her hands are so crooked with arthritis, knobbly and yet thin, like a bird's claws. She still wears all her rings.

"I get very tired sometimes," she said, her eyes not sure who I was.

"That's all right," I told her, not letting myself cry again. "Sleep if you like. I don't mind."

"Will you be here?" she asked, like a small child afraid of the dark.

"I'll stay as long as I can," I said.

She was asleep again when the nurse came in. "There's only ten minutes left till Visiting Hours are over," she told me. "You might just as well run along now. The poor old thing doesn't know much of anything most of the time. Mind you, she can get in a temper when we're trying to get her washed or fed, but usually she's right out of the picture."

I wanted to jump up and slap her. I sat where I was, holding the knotted yet frail hand with its too big rings.

"She knows everything," I whispered, "and she is *not* a poor old thing, she is a distinguished lady."

The nurse laughed.

"Have it your own way," she said, not unkindly, and left.

I stayed till the bell went. Mrs. Thurstone was still asleep when I had to leave her. I kissed her cheek very lightly. I'd never have done it if she had been awake. Perhaps I will next time I go.

All the way home, I noticed the beauty of the new snow. And I could feel our two hands linked, giving strength to each other.

Who You Are

Today Miss McIntyre, who teaches us Guidance, said, "You have to decide who you are and where you're going."

Sounds simple. Just decide. I think it *is* simple for Emily. She's Emily Blair, daughter of the Manager of the Royal Bank, member of the Presbyterian Church, high achiever in school, sister of Louisa. And she knows where she's going — or she thinks she does. She wants to teach Grade One. She's out of her mind. Only... maybe not....

I could do that about me too, of course. There are labels that partly fit. I too am the child of my parents, except I'm beginning to see that Mother and Dad are not just my parents, the way I used to think. They are separate people with thoughts of their own. Sometimes they seem like strangers. I don't belong to a church. I'm Jewish — but I don't know, yet, what being Jewish is going to mean to me.

That's not what I'm talking about though, or it's only one part of it. I want to find out how important it is, my being Jewish, but I'd like to be everything else too. And nothing else.

I'd like to teach Grade Five but I want to write a symphony and live in a lighthouse and fly an airplane. I'd like to own an orchard or keep bees. I'd like to be a policewoman and I've thought about being a nun. I think I'll write books... I sound like a little kid.

There are so many roads though. I can't write a symphony, I know that. And I'm pretty sure I'd never make it as a nun. But I just might keep bees, if I really wanted to. Except... what about my lighthouse?

Right now I could be anybody, Miss McIntyre. Can't you understand that? I could be anybody at all.

I'm not ready to choose and besides, I'm choosing more than one road. I'm putting myself together, Miss McIntyre. But it is like a jigsaw puzzle. I keep on finding new pieces.

If you were once a puzzle, you soon found the edge pieces and fitted yourself inside. There is no edge to me yet. I hope the picture turns out to be worth the work. I hope I never discover an edge.

Yesterday

Yesterday I knew all the answers
Or I knew my parents did.

Yesterday I had my Best Friend
And my Second Best Friend
And I knew whose Best Friend I was
And who disliked me.

Yesterday I hated asparagus and coconut and parsnips
And mustard pickles and olives
And anything I'd never tasted.

Yesterday I knew what was Right and what was Wrong
And I never had any trouble deciding which was which.
It always seemed so obvious.

But today...everything's changing.
I suddenly have a million unanswered questions.
Everybody I meet might become a friend.
I tried eating snails with garlic sauce — and I liked them!
And I know the delicate shadings that lie between
Good and evil — and I face their dilemma.
Life is harder now...and yet, easier...
And more and more exciting!